esther deans' gardening book
growing without digging

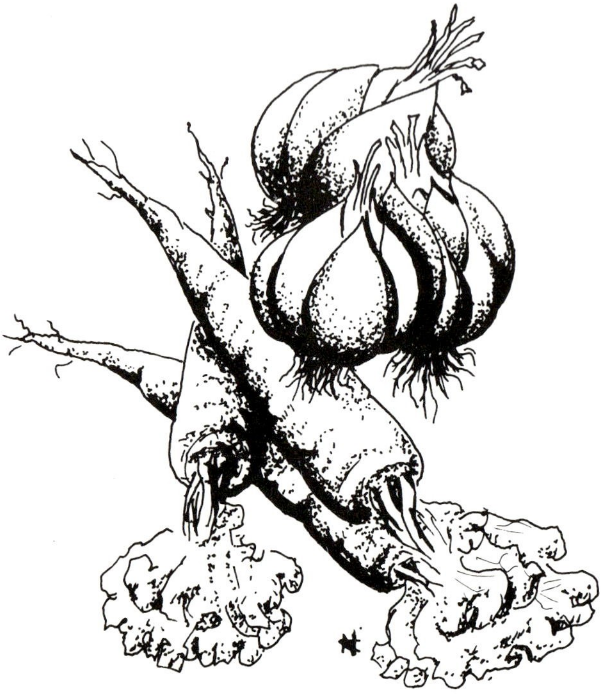

esther deans' gardening book
growing without digging

Harper & Row (Australasia) Pty. Ltd.
Sydney • New York • San Francisco • London

Harper & Row (Australasia) Pty. Ltd.
Sydney • New York • San Francisco • London

Created & Produced by Obelisk Press Pty. Ltd. NSW
First Published in Australia 1977
First Impression November 1977
Second Impression December 1977
Third Impression January 1978
Fourth Impression 1979
Fifth Impression 1980
Sixth Impression 1980
Seventh Impression 1981
Eighth Impression 1982
Ninth Impression 1983
Tenth Impression 1984
Eleventh Impression 1985
Copyright © 1977 Esther Deans
Printed and bound in Singapore by
Kyodo Shing Loong Printing Industries
All rights reserved
ISBN 06 312 0011

contents

foreword. 7

1. esther deans
 and home gardening. 8

2. a garden of paper,
 straw & hay. 16

3. seed & soil selection
 the pendulum method. 28

4. companion planting
 & pest control. 34

5. comfrey
 & other herbs. 40

6. fertilizing, compost
 & home made liquids. 46

This book is dedicated to the spastic children
who cannot run on the soft warm earth,
and to the blind children who cannot see
the wonders of creation.

foreword

Esther Deans' no-dig garden has been an inspiration to so many people, showing them how to grow plants and how to enjoy them, not by battling with Mother Nature but by co-operating with her. They have discovered peace and happiness in the garden by accepting nature as a friend rather than an opposing force.

Some practices I do not understand, perhaps because there is at this stage no accepted scientific explanation for them, but they are producing results without involving much effort or expense.

The no-dig principle I accept fully. I have for many years protested that it is so wrong to bury living soil. Healthy surface soil is certainly alive, teeming with organisms busily converting organic matter into plant foods. Some of these useful organisms also inhibit or prevent development of parasitic fungi responsible for plant disease.

In nature, spent plant material or other organic waste is deposited on the soil surface. Obviously the great population of microscopic creatures concerned with the recycling of organic material was also intended to live in or on the surface soil, not at spade depth.

Our friends the earthworms with their constant tunnelling will supply the aeration needed by plant roots in any healthy soil receiving a continuous supply of organic matter. Earthworms also extend the depth of top soil by pulling decomposed organic material to lower depths and bringing soil from lower levels to the surface.

Esther Deans explains how to start a successful hay and straw garden on the surface of the toughest soil, at the same time improving the latter. This most unconventional type of garden can even be started on solid concrete. Hoping that you find the key to more successful and happier gardening in this book.

Allan Seale

1. esther deans & home gardening

Why do we want to have a garden? I believe it is the Love of growing things, of watching the wonders of Nature unfold before our eyes. To see the fascinating results of a tiny seed yielding its beauty in colour, form and fragrance. Fragrance in many forms: sweet perfume from the tiny violet, the honey smell, the delightful culinary scent of herbs. We so often pass by without thinking of these wonders. The brilliance of the red poinsettia, the soft glorious blue of the jacaranda tree, the bright yellow of the daffodil.

Rest for a while in your garden and let your thoughts wander at random to ponder on its beauty. You will be surprised at how relaxed you will feel after a short time. Think of the creatures we find in our gardens — the beauty of the butterfly; the swift flight of the birds, the joy of hearing them chatter and sing; the minute insects under stones and plants; our hardworking friend the earthworm; and even the caterpillar who enjoys eating our tender plants!

Many books have been written about home gardens, compost gardens, organic gardens, bio-dynamic gardens, hydroponic gardens, and so on. In this book I want to talk of the most important of all: a garden made with Love, with a capital "L". A garden of vital and healthy plants to provide food for our own health. Hippocrates stressed the importance of good taste and variety: "If the musician composed a piece of music all on one note, it would fail to please."

The same applies to our food. We should eat as great a variety of natural, fresh, unprocessed food, especially fruit and vegetables, so that over seven days our mineral and vitamin intake pleases our body and gives us the good health to enjoy a full and active life. The home garden is Nature's answer!

My gardening philosophy is that one should be able to enjoy the results of successful vegetable growing, as well as other plants, without tiresome "spade" work. Gardens are not made by sitting in the shade and saying, "Oh how beautiful!", but neither need they be made with hours of backbreaking toil. The actual construction of my kind of garden is described in this book, and is simplicity

BELOW:
It is the fragrance as well as beauty that makes a garden a wonderful experience.

itself. But briefly, the garden is made on top of the existing ground, using newspaper, lucerne hay, straw and compost. It does not require any digging to build, or to maintain. Given the right conditions, Nature is only too pleased to do most of the work for you. This garden can be made and enjoyed by old people, the handicapped, as well as all of those whose busy daily program does not allow them the time to spend hours in the backyard.

A usual question asked of me when speaking to a group of gardeners either at home or at a meeting is, "What made you start a garden like this?" Maybe it will help you not to be discouraged about a poor sick garden if I tell you the story.

BELOW:
Over 4,500 people have visited the garden. A typical Saturday group excited about new possibilities.

Some years ago I was very ill, almost bedridden, and many items of food were wrong for me. My body was not getting enough of the correct nourishment. At the time we had only one vegetable garden of imported sandy loam. How like my own life it was — sick and undernourished. My love of the earth and growing things began to come back to me. I could feel the need to start gardening and decided to try to regain my health through eating as many home-grown vegetables as possible. Exercising in the sun and rain and contact with the earth has worked wonders for me.

The old garden was quite depleted of humus and the white grubs had so multiplied that they presented a real problem. The Department of Agriculture advised poison to eradicate them, but by this time I had learned about poisons and their injurious effect on our gardens, so I gently worked the soil until all the grubs had gone. It came repeatedly to my mind that I should use lucerne hay, remembering what I had read years before about the wonderful qualities of this plant. As lucerne grows, its deep roots bring up from the earth minerals, trace elements and other valuable nutriments which make the hay useful to the plants in our garden. I ordered some from the local produce store. When the man came to deliver the first bale of lucerne hay to me, he looked around the garden for the horse! When told that it was for the garden, he stared at me with a very questioning gaze. Many bales have been delivered uneventfully since that day.

I covered the area of the garden to be restored with the pads of lucerne hay as they came from the bale, gathered some earthworms to put beneath the pads, spread a little compost over the top and started watering. It wasn't long before the earthworms began to work in the hay and multiply. For six weeks we watched this area and then planted bean seeds. The results were splendid. Encouraged, I started on the next section, restoring the remainder of the garden in the same manner.

This was the genesis of my NO-DIG GARDEN! A garden is something to be enjoyed and shared. Over the years much knowledge has been gained by experiments. We are learning and improving all the time, hence the garden described to you in this book is different (and easier) than the original prototype of many years ago. I have graduated from "L-Plates" but am still on "P-Plates", always discovering new and wonderful things.

In fact, the experiences that have flowed into my life as a direct result of success with my garden, have literally changed the way I live. So many wonderful and

BELOW:
I have progressed from "L" plates but I am still on "P" plates, always discovering new and wonderful things.

49½ lbs in 24 square feet of potatoes

1. Put the potatoes in a little compost on the hay, under the straw.
   The green tops push up through the straw.

2. Lift the straw to check on the progress of the potatoes.

3. Washing for storage is not necessary.

4. A bumper crop! 49½ lb from an area 4' × 6'.

enriching things have occurred. The initial success of the first garden I built according to the plan in this book, that is, the first one after the prototype I have just described, was most encouraging. The best yield from it was 49½ pounds weight of potatoes from an area measuring 8 feet long by 6 feet wide—48 square feet, and this was from one planting!

Members of a local gardening club heard from a friend about my garden and expressed a wish to come and see it. I was delighted that they were interested and after their visit word of mouth spread and more requests were received not only from gardening clubs, but Senior Citizens' Clubs, Ladies Auxiliaries and the like. It seemed that people were interested. I started a Visitors' Book to keep a record

of my visitors. As more people found out about my methods, I found myself writing small articles for magazines in response to requests from editors. The project gained momentum. My garden was visited by reporters, written about in newspapers and more magazines. I was asked to speak on gardening programs on the radio and a number of television segments have been made on the garden in both Australia and New Zealand. Perhaps the biggest thrill was when I was visited by a radio journalist who broadcast on Radio Australia short wave. We spent a long time talking, he signed the Visitors' Book and left. Imagine when a friend rang me at 6 a.m. one morning to say that he had just heard an international broadcast in which there was a segment about my GARDEN WITHOUT DIGGING. I was happy to

BELOW:
talking with garden expert Alan Seale for one of his television programmes.

share something which had brought me such happiness and health.

I first opened the garden in 1975; there have been visitors to it ever since. 1975 was the year that I was awarded the Championship Ribbon for vegetables at the Ku-Ring-Gai Horticultural Society Show, as well as 1st and 2nd Prizes for two dahlias I had entered. There is an amusing story about the dahlias. As I was picking the vegetables on the morning of the show I noticed two exquisite dahlias growing among the vegetables. I like to have flowers in the vegetable garden for colour, and of course it brings the bees who are pollinators. On a whim, I picked the two dahlias and decided to enter them.

Arriving at the show there were many flower exhibitors ushering in their best examples, all protected in boxes against the wind and looking very practised and professional. There was I simply marching in with two flowers in a plain vase. I entered the flowers first and then went off to attend to the business of entering all of the vegetables which were in a different sections. After the judging, I was so excited at the success of the vegetables that I forgot about the dahlias. I was overwhelmed that the two flowers I had plonked in vases on the spur of the moment had done so well.

BELOW:
Dahlias are a delightful flower. They bring a gladness to my garden.

BELOW:
Prizes won at Ku-ring-gai Horticultural Society Show in 1975.

Since that day in 1975, when I opened the garden as a result of success at the Show, more than 4,500 people have signed the Visitors' Book. This garden has now been built by hundreds of people around Australia and overseas. The photographs here were sent to me by a man who lives in a suburb close to mine, showing the amazing results he achieved with his first garden.

The greatest success story comes from a lady who also lives in Sydney. She visited my garden one weekend and was excited by the prospect of being able to raise such wonderful vegetables without tiresome work. We talked at length about the methods of building the garden and she left determined to try her own hand at it. The results were incredible to say the least: During the first season of her NO-DIG garden, she produced 200 pounds weight of zucchini and button squash!

This was just too much for the family to eat, so she made enquiries at the local health food shop with the result that she was able to supply them with vegetables to sell to others. She had actually made a commercially viable vegetable market garden in her own back yard, and one which left her with still enough free time to run the house and enjoy other activities as well. I wonder how many other market gardens there are like that, which can be established and yield so much in the first season!

It is now a total of 11 years since I started the first garden: how wonderful they have been. A similar picture to one who is having music lessons—slowly at first, A, B, C, then with more practice and learning (and a few mistakes!) one becomes more expert. Finally after constant practice, you appear on the concert platform.

It is good to feel a little emotion at such an achievement—then to be asked to share your knowledge and experience with those who have not yet reached this goal.

It has been an enormous satisfaction for me. There are many people whose lives could be enriched by sharing something good. Sharing is caring. Many wonderful people have crossed my path to add another chapter to my life. To all those who have shared my garden with me I say thank you. For without them I would not have had this exciting, stimulating, interesting and happy life.

OPPOSITE:
A rich harvest of vegetables without tiresome work. This friend produced 200 pounds of zucchini and button squash in her first attempt. The garden was placed among the rocks on an embankment.

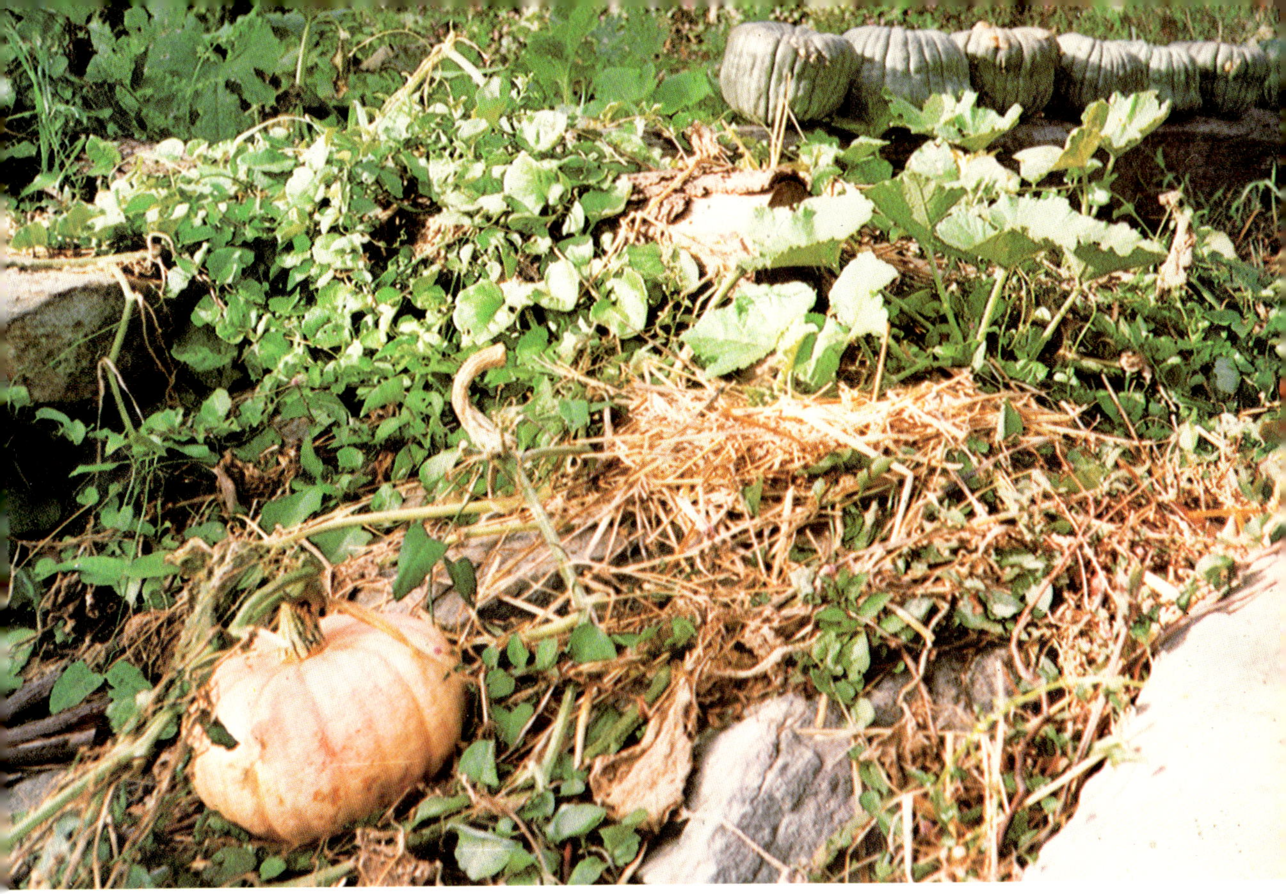

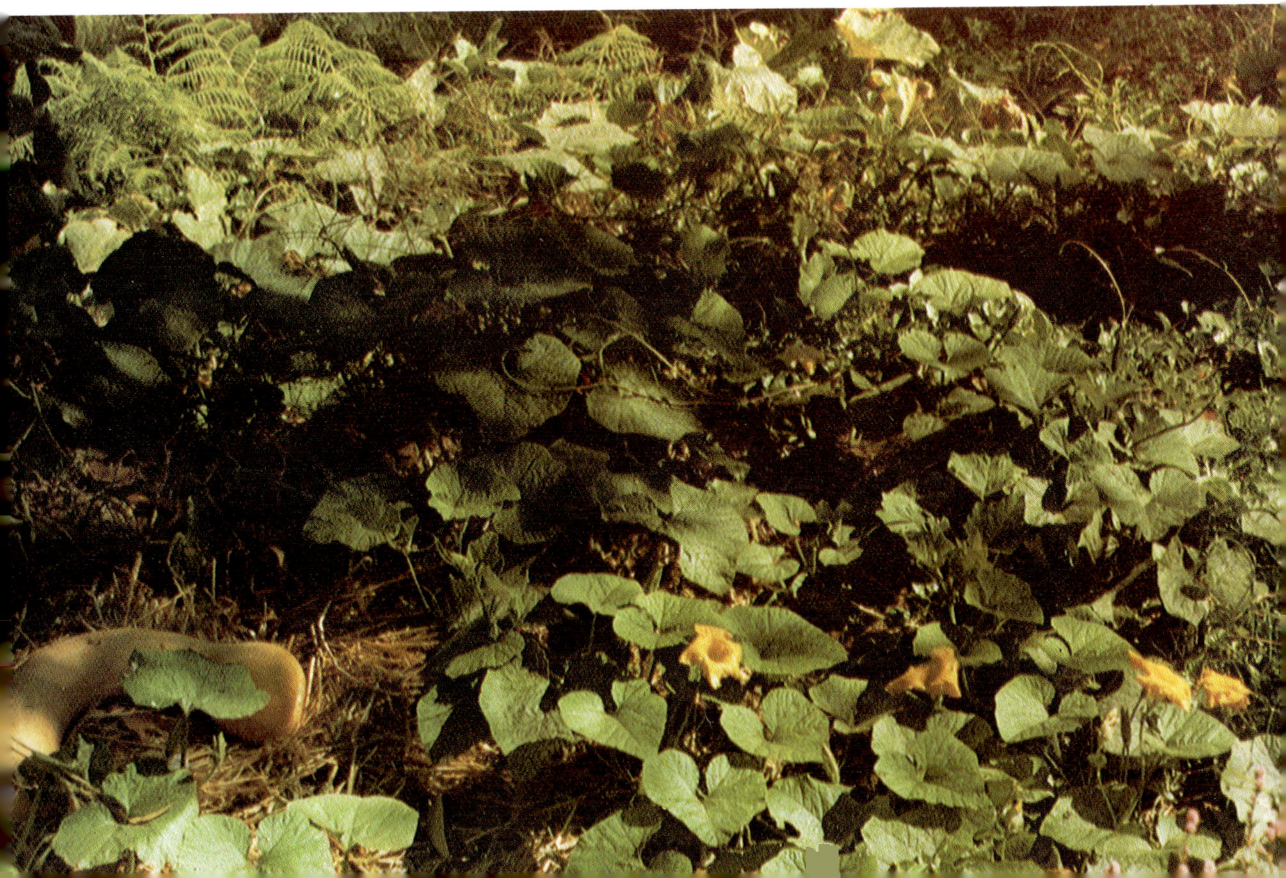

2. a garden of paper, straw & hay

how to build it

Mine is simply a backyard vegetable garden, divided into several beds and maintained using organic principles. It is made without toil, without digging, without sweat and is easy enough for a child or old person to build. In fact it is so easy that a handicapped person or one in a wheelchair can build, maintain and enjoy a slightly modified version of this garden, but more about that later. For the moment, the design of the basic garden.

The idea is to build a garden on top of the existing ground. The "GARDEN WITHOUT DIGGING" comprises rectangular beds raised above ground level, formed with old pieces of hardboard, small concrete clip bricks or anything to hold the rich organic mixture in place. The garden can be built for two types of environment: one to go on top of hard, rocky ground, or concrete, the other to put on a piece of lawn or existing garden. For a garden on top of lawn or existing garden, select a sunny spot and spread a layer of newspaper a good ¼ inch deep. Make sure the newspaper is well overlapped to prevent the lawn from growing through. Do not use coloured paper or cardboard.

Cover the newspaper with pads of lucerne hay (as it comes from the bale). Over this layer sprinkle a light dusting of organic fertilizer or dry poultry manure. Cover this with a layer about 8 inches deep of loose straw and sprinkle again with the same fertilizer. Finally on top put a patch of good compost, 3 to 4 inches deep and about 18 inches across, where seeds are to be planted. One bale of lucerne hay and one bale of straw make a good-sized garden.

ABOVE:
Lucerne hay and straw used to make the garden.

If you are making the garden on top of hard, rocky ground, or on top of concrete, the very first layer you should put down is one of old leaves, small sticks and pieces of seaweed, to a depth of three or four inches. On top of this place a layer of newspaper, and continue to build as described above. See how easy it really is!

planting

Now you are ready to plant the seeds. I like to make this garden at the end of August, when it is the season to plant summer vegetables such as zucchini, cucumber, squash and pumpkin. At the other end of the garden I plant about 8 potatoes on the lucerne hay (i.e. under the straw) with a little compost around each one. This gives me an ideal situation for the rotation of crops: alternating a leafy crop with a root vegetable and vice versa. For instance, one follows potato with cabbage. Water the garden after planting the seeds and then according to need, keeping the straw just damp.

Many people have made this garden at different times of the year, planting seedlings, and had success. You should experiment and have fun in your garden.

After a few months, at the finish of the leafy summer crops, the layers of the garden will have composted down and melted into each other, and now the ground is ready for the second crop which will be productive during the winter months. *No digging is needed.* You just add a layer of compost or manure and plant your seeds of turnips, carrots, onions, spinach, cauliflower or cabbage.

Plant the vegetables in patches rather than rows and remember to rotate the crop!

ABOVE:
The garden composts down and the layers melt into each other.

constructing the garden

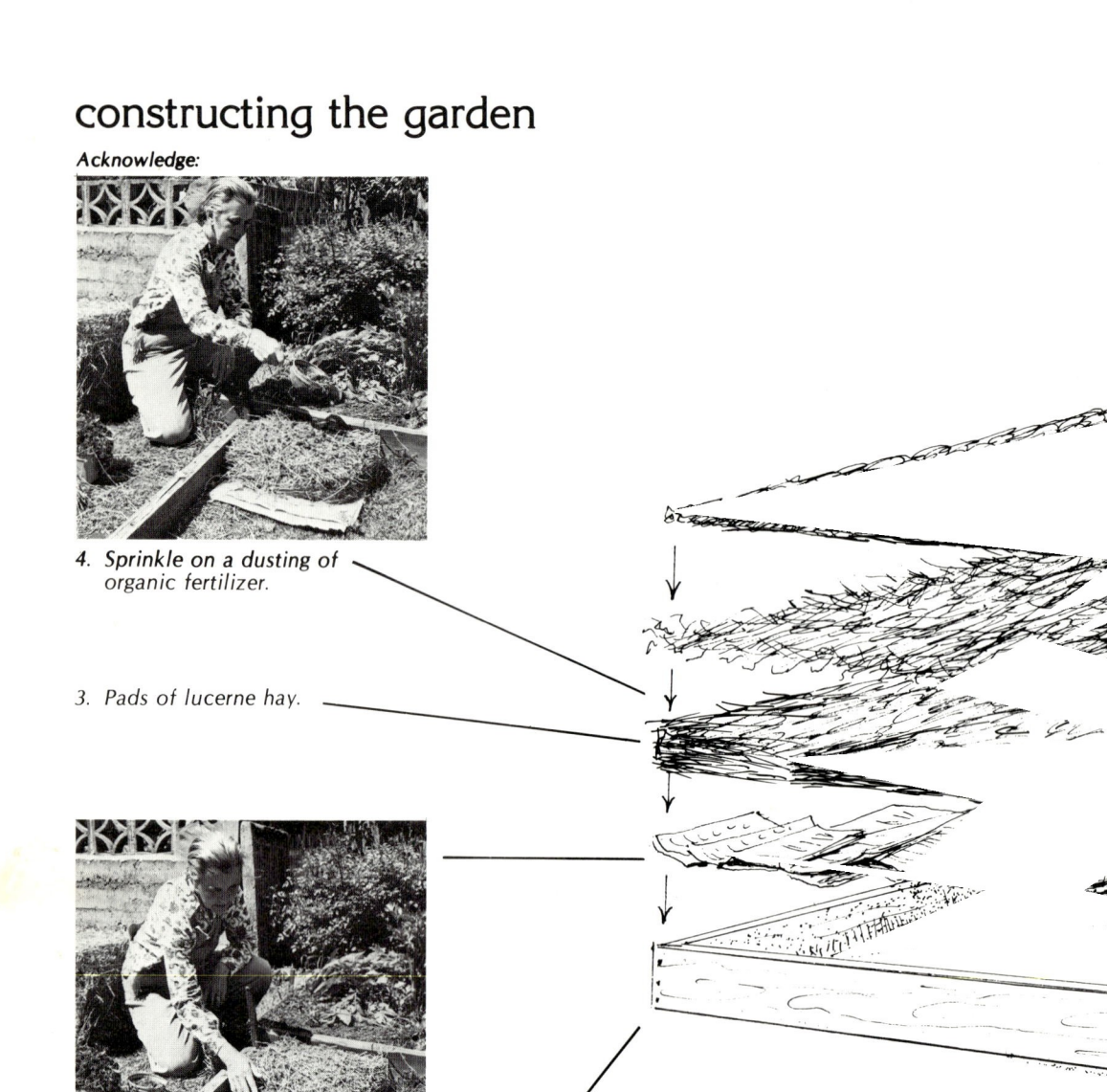

Acknowledge:

4. Sprinkle on a dusting of organic fertilizer.

3. Pads of lucerne hay.

2. A layer of newspapers (¼ in, ½ cm) Thick.

1. Build a box with boards or bricks.

Ed Ramsay

7. Tip a circle of rich compost 3-4in (10cm) deep and about 18in (45cm) across where seeds are to be planted.

6. Sprinkle this layer with some fertilizer.

5. Cover with about 8in (20cm) of loose straw.

Potatoes can be grown in this garden throughout the year—make smaller sowings. As the potatoes swell make sure they are well covered with straw to prevent "greening" which poisons the potato. Do not dig when taking them up but simply part the straw and collect your delicious potatoes—no washing necessary. During the winter months I covered the small area with a piece of hessian; results excellent.

Cabbage should be planted following a root crop, sugar loaf or superette are my first favourite for a small garden and will grow all year. Chinese cabbage and red cabbage are a must for the delicious coleslaw needed in our diet. Grow several sage plants in your cabbage patch, as they help to repel white cabbage moths and other insects.

Tomatoes are a wonderful vegetable and should be planted following root crops, and with care they can be picked from Christmas until the end of June. The first seedlings planted at the end of August should give first picking by Christmas. The second planting of seedlings in February will give a good late crop. When the weather is cold during the night, cover the whole plant with a long dry cleaning plastic bag, which makes an ideal little glass house. Take the lower leaves off the tomato plant, leaving only the last 25cm of leaves on the top. Grow a variety of herbs amongst them: chives, parsley, basil and French marigolds make a pretty useful border around the bed.

Beans are a good vegetable and will grow happily in any well-drained good soil. Do not give them too much nitrogen as this makes the leaves "heavy". They need plenty of water during the hot weather, but you must take care not to water onto the leaves during the heat and intense sunshine of the middle of the day. Wait until the sun has gone down. If water is needed during the day, use a watering can and direct the stream around the plant on

OPPOSITE:
(Photographs continued on pages 24 and 25)
These pictures were sent by a man showing how he put the garden down and the results. In the top picture note the newspapers in one garden and the hay in the next. In the bottom picture the straw has been added to one garden while stakes are being placed in the other so as not to tear the newspaper.

BELOW:
Here I am picking part of a huge crop of broadbeans. Seeds from the largest pods will be kept for next season's plantings.

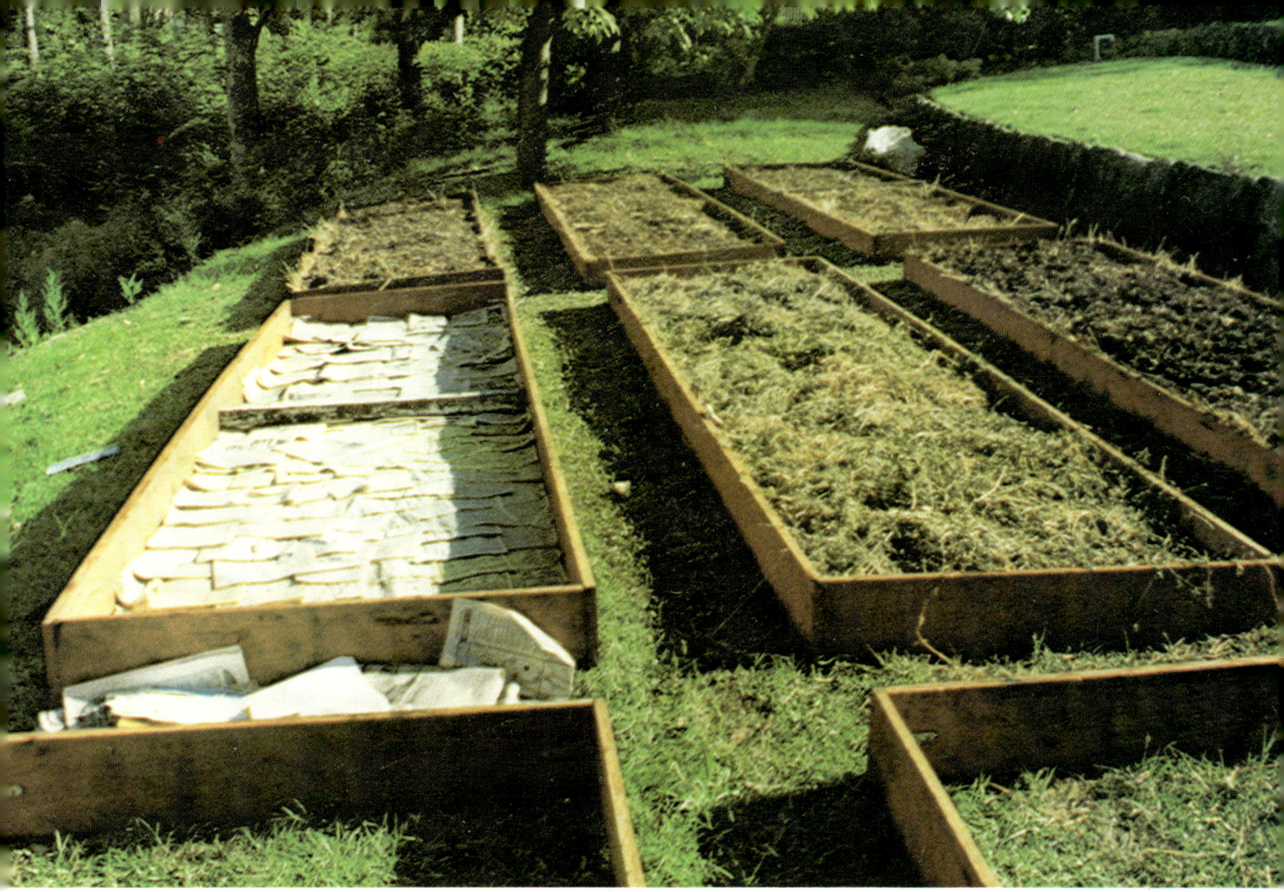

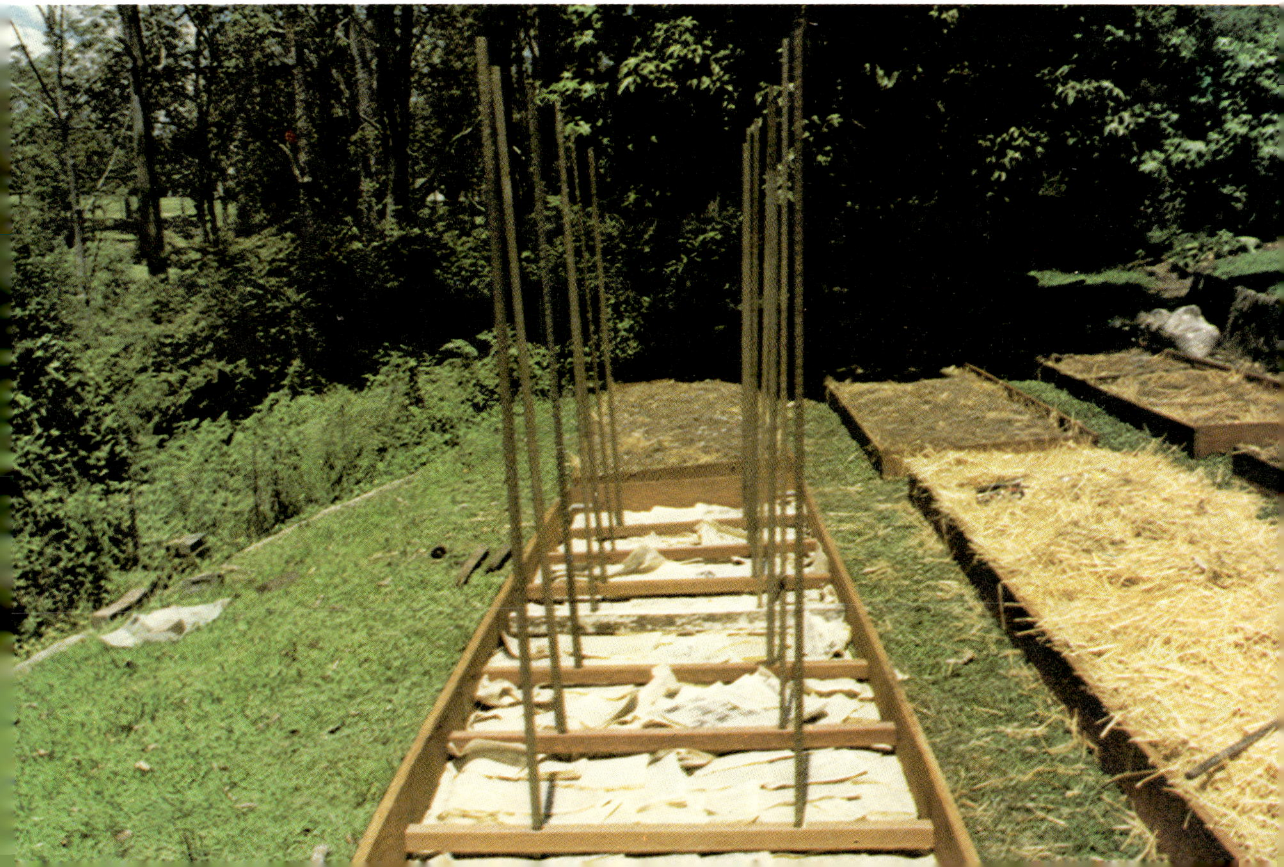

the ground—not on the leaves. In cold weather it is best to water them in the morning. This entire watering program applies to all vegetables and for best results you should follow it.

Carrots and parsnips can be ready for picking every two months if the seeds are planted regularly in small patches. In very hot weather assist germination by covering the seeds with newspaper and keeping the earth moist underneath. At the first sign of germination remove the newspaper. Keep the ground moist and treat parsnips in the same way.

Sweet corn is a must in my garden. With a little planning you can expect three crops during the year instead of one. Plant only positive seeds, the first sowing being in September, the second in November, the third in January.

Celery is a worthwhile addition to the garden. You should try to eat some every day. The general opinion is that it is difficult to germinate, but this is not so when the soil is rich and healthy. I allow my best plants to go to seed, because good seed means a good plant.

Broad beans are another excellent and prolific vegetable. Plant first, second and third crops and make small sowings each time, which ensures pickings over several weeks. When the plants are beginning to bloom, the young tips from the top of the plant may be picked and used as vegetable. Also the pod, when finger length, is delicioius when steamed whole.

Potatoes are a rewarding home garden crop when grown in small patches: they can supply potatoes all the year through. Growing them in the straw garden has proved a very interesting experiment and has produced a potato with first class keeping qualities. No heavy digging or washing is necessary before storing.

Choko is a very handy vine—a good positive plant will remain productive for a long time. A negative vine will grow and look beautiful but the fruit is absent. So the mystery is solved when we know how to test our seeds and plants. The ideal way to grow choko is to have a free-standing frame well away from neighbours' trees and fences, etc.

Pumpkins need plenty of room and are an excellent vegetable to grow because of their good keeping properties. I have had them to 17 pounds in weight! They can attract lots of pests and the slugs and snails love to make the most of the shade and moisture beneath the leaves. We will talk later about pest control.

Cucumbers make a good addition to summer menus—when home grown they are much nicer in flavour and quality. There are several varieties, all of them being good to eat. The cucumber likes fertile conditions—see the section on fertilizers.

Beetroot is so nutritious—both the bulb and the leaf. They like plenty of food when growing, particularly liquid seaweed and liquid poultry manure.

elevated garden

Another exciting possibility occurred to me. Could the NO-DIG garden be made or modified for disabled gardeners? Many suggestions were offered, some of them expensive, some of them requiring a great deal of labour and hard work. Then I decided to try to build the garden on top of an old bedstead. It sounded ideal — little expense was involved, the height of the bedstead was correct for people in wheelchairs or for those who were unable to stoop down to ground level.

First, we placed it in a position where the wheelchair could move right around it without hindrance, and which received plenty of sun. The next step was to build sides onto it, which was easy using old hardboards and pieces of masonite — offcuts about 15cm high which were wired and bound around the sides, foot and head. We lined this "trough" with plastic. The liner was secured into the corners and several holes made in it for drainage. Finally a couple of old fence palings were laid on top of the plastic. The garden could now be built in layers as described, following the recipe for hard, rocky ground.

Zucchini and cucumber seeds were planted in the middle, four potato seeds at the foot, and some carrots at the head. The cucumbers eventually draped over the side and some really first class zucchini made the experiment totally worthwhile. The follow-on crop was lettuce, endive, chinese spinach, a few marigolds and heartsease for colour.

Another bed is currently being prepared to try strawberries; experimentation is such excellent therapy! One lady who came to visit my garden was most excited to see the bed being used. Immediately she saw the possibility for a "three-decker" garden using an old double-decker bunk for two lucerne hay and straw gardens, and a smaller bed underneath for herbs. This of course is wonderful for garden lovers who have a very limited area, particularly in the inner city suburbs.

BELOW:
Made on an old bed this garden flourishes. People who have difficulty stooping or who are confined to the wheelchair find this exciting. This same method can be applied on terraces or other confined areas.

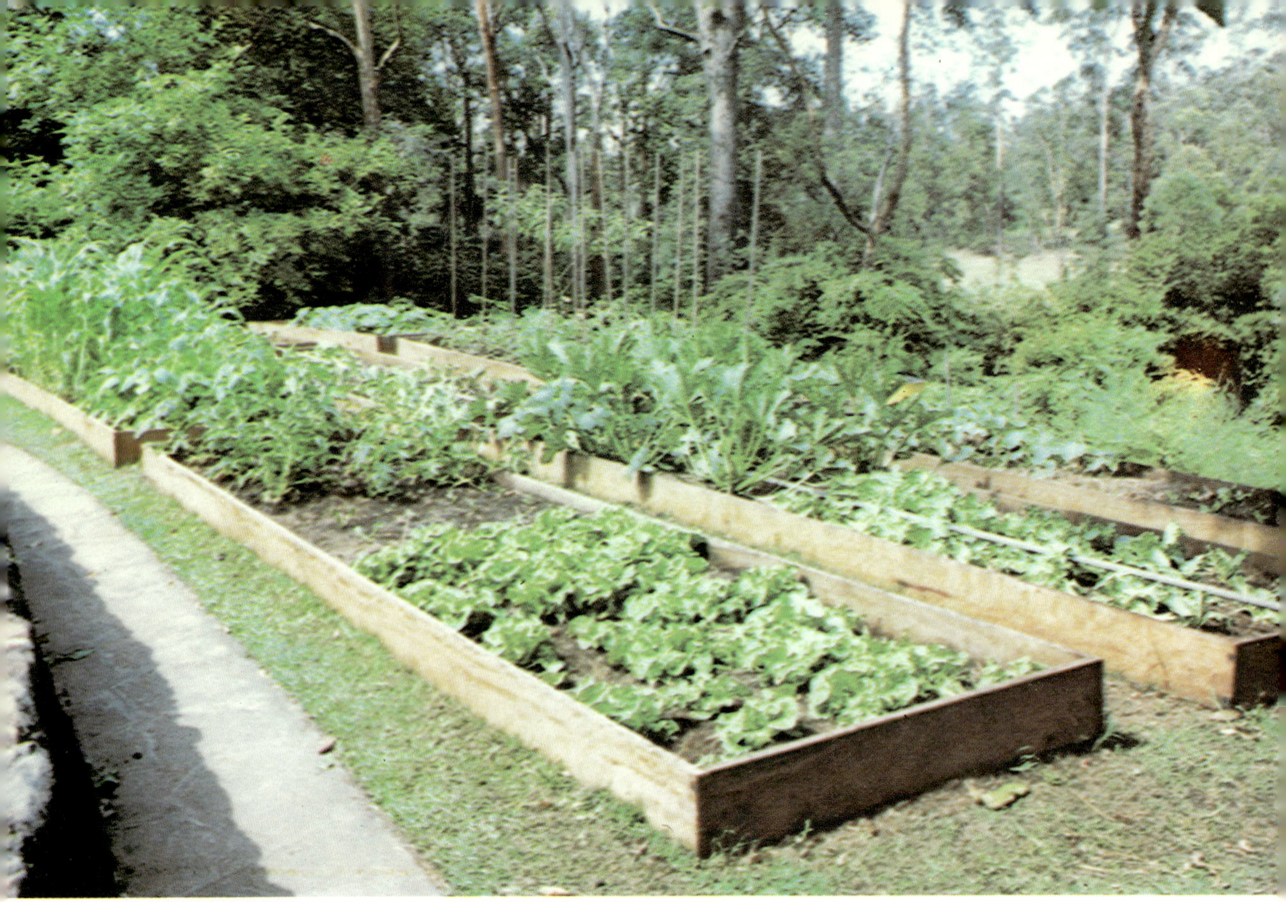

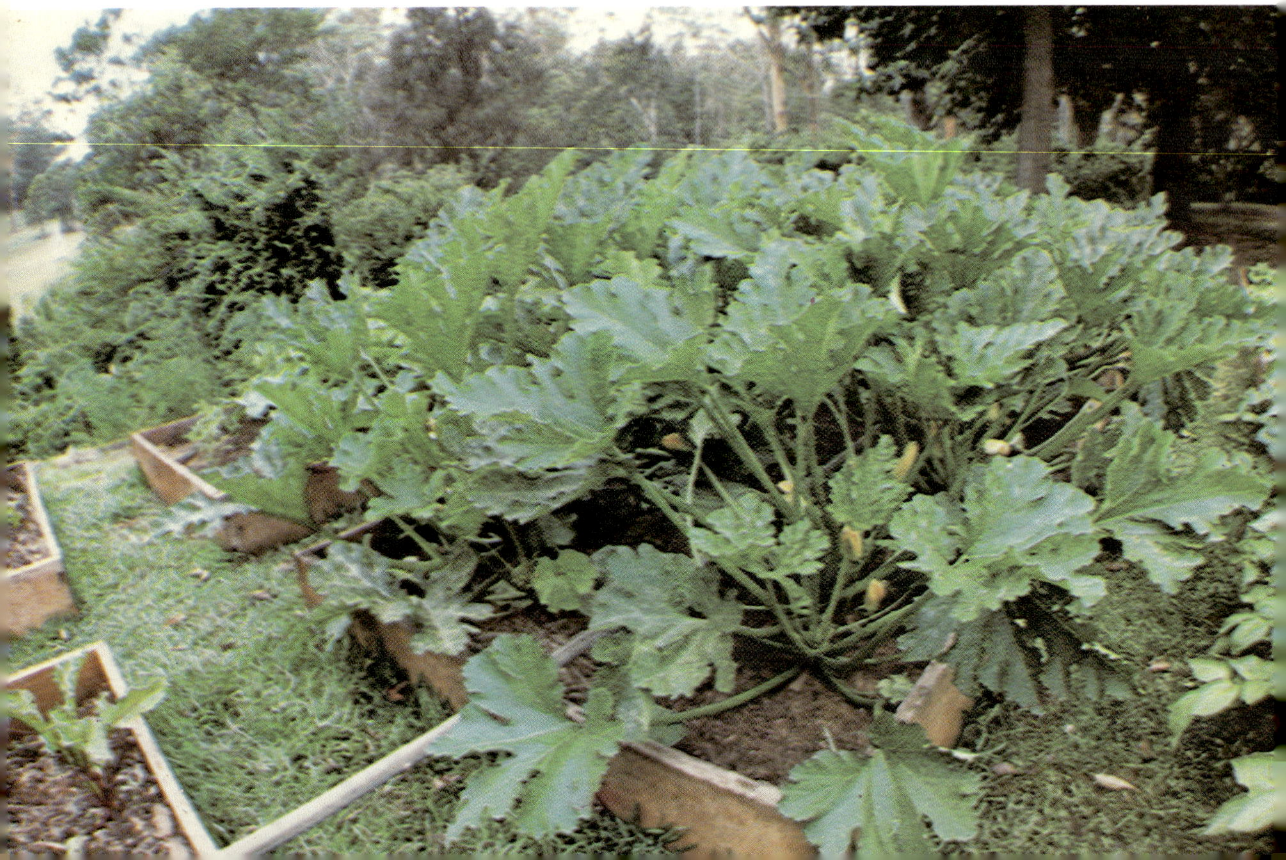

sowing guide

Once the garden is established, that is, after the first season, this should be your VEGETABLE SOWING GUIDE FOR TEMPERATE CLIMATES.

january

SOW SEEDS OF—all beans, cucumbers, brussels sprouts, cauliflower, cabbage, radish, lettuce, tomato.

february

SOW SEEDS OF—white turnips, all beans, beetroot, lettuce, carrots, celery, endive, leeks, marrow, onions, silver beet, radish, zucchini, sweet corn.
PLANT SEEDLINGS OF—broccoli, cabbage, lettuce, chinese cabbage, cauliflower.

A continuation of the garden on page 21. These pictures show the results. The straw and hay have composted down and abundant growth is evident.

march
broadbeans, peas, carrots, celery, chinese cabbage, chives, cress, endive, herbs, kohlrabi, lettuce, mustard, onion, peas, radish, shallots, spinach, turnips.

april
broadbeans, cabbage, chinese cabbage, chives, cress, endive, herbs, kohlrabi, lettuce, mustard, onions, peas, radish, shallots, spinach, turnips.

may
broadbeans, cabbage, chives, cress, endive, herbs, kohlrabi, onions, peas, radish, shallots, spinach, turnip.

june
broadbeans, cabbage, chives, cress, endive, herbs, kohlrabi, onions, peas, radish, rhubarb.

july
beetroot, broadbeans, carrots, lettuce, mustard, onion.

august
beetroot, carrots, chinese cabbage, chives, endive, herbs, kohlrabi, leek, lettuce, onions, parsley, parsnips, peas, radish, rhubarb, shallots, silver beet, spinach.

september
climbing beans, dwarf beans, beetroot, cabbage, capsicum, carrots, chinese cabbage, chives, cress, cucumber, egg plant, endive, herbs, kohlrabi, leek, lettuce, bush marrow, rock melon, water melon, mustard cress, parsley, parsnips, peas, bush pumpkin, running pumpkin, radish, rhubarb, shallots, silver beet, spinach, squash, sweet corn, tomatoes.

october & november
climbing beans, dwarf beans, beetroot, cabbage, capsicum, carrots, celery, chinese cabbage, chives, cress, cucumber, egg plant, endive, herbs, leek, lettuce, bush marrow, rock melon, water melon, mustard, parsley, parsnips, peas, bush pumpkin, running pumpkin, radish, rhubarb, shallots, silver beet, spinach, bush squash, sweet corn, tomatoes.

december
climbing beans, dwarf beans, beetroot, broccoli, brussels sprouts, cabbage, capsicum, carrots, cauliflower, celery, cress, cucumber, egg plant, endive, herbs, leek, lettuce, bush marrow, rock melon, water melon, mustard cress, parsley, parsnips, bush pumpkin, running pumpkin, radish, silver beet, bush squash, running squash, sweet corn, tomatoes.

Consult your local nurseryman as to what is suitable to grow in your particular area and climate. Again I cannot stress too much the importance of crop rotation. By alternating the type of plants grown, one keeps the soil in good condition and produces healthier plants.

maintaining the garden

One of the most important things about the NO-DIG garden is just that—DON'T DIG IT! Digging this garden can spoil the wonderful work that Nature is doing for you. Our friends the earthworms do a wonderful job of cultivating the soil and do not like to be disturbed, so let them work in peace. It is easy to maintain the fertility of the garden by rotating the crop and adding when necessary compost, cow manure, liquid manure, lucerne hay, etc.

Watering the garden is an important duty. The general rule is that the plants should not be watered while the sun is shining at full strength. The best times are early in the morning in winter, and in the evening during the summer. If you go away on holidays or for some other reason are unable to water the garden, then place plenty of mulch around the plants and water well before you go. Do not mind if a few weeds spring up as they can be helpful binding the soil together and so preventing a wash out in heavy rain.

Weeding the NO-DIG garden is easy. Because the garden is built up from nothing using lucerne hay, straw, paper and compost, there are no weeds initially and it is simply a matter of pulling up the baby weeds as they appear. "Keeping pace" with the weeds in this fashion and pulling out a few each day keeps the situation under control. However, I do not recommend that you remove all of the weeds. Leave some growing, particularly around the edges as I have mentioned, to bind the soil so that it will not wash away during a downpour. Weeds are helpful in this way and a few won't destroy the garden or rob the plants of too much nutrition.

BELOW:
It is important not to dig this garden. I use this small fork for quickly removing any unwanted weeds.

3. seed & soil selection
the pendulum method

> "Behold, I have given you every herb bearing seed which is upon the face of the earth, and every tree, in which is the fruit of a tree yielding seed; to you it shall be for meat..." GENESIS 1:29

Once we have established the soil for our garden the other basis for its success is the seeds.

Seeds, both small and large, each hold in their case a wonder of creation. From the acorn the oak tree; from tiny celery seeds beautiful green stalks with their source of health giving minerals.

Hold in your fingers the seed of an oleander. The brown velvety seed is topped with an umbrella of silken threads to enable it to float and land on some fertile spot to grow. No man's hand is needed to plant it.

There is a special joy in planting seeds and eventually watching the young green sprouts push out of the soil; the beginning of a plant.

Some years ago I was given a carob bean which had come from the Middle East. Knowing very little about carob trees I decided to plant the brown seed and wait. What a rich reward has come! Watching it grow over the years has been an interesting lesson. It has grown into a very lovely tree about 4 metres high. As yet no fruit has appeared. The food value of the carob bean is very high. One full bean will sustain a sheep for a whole day. It has a delicious caramel flavour and its high food value makes it satisfying to chew.

BELOW:
My carob tree in full glory.

In my own kitchen I have not used cocoa for years, substituting it with carob powder. The bean is large, brown in colour and quite sweet.

Although it is a little like cocoa to look at the food value is vastly different. The bean contains good natural carbohydrate, potassium, silicon, iron and a number of trace elements, as well as a considerable amount of the B-group vitamins, thiamine, riboflavin and niacin. It is rich in pectin, contains 7% protein and very little fat.

In 1967 I had in my garden two very healthy paw paw plants about 1 metre high. I always understood it was necessary to have a male and a female plant before one could expect a crop of fruit, but how could I find the answer? A chance visit of a friend enabled me to learn how to tell the difference.

Whilst walking around the garden I expressed a wish to learn how to sex paw paw. My friend said, "I think I can help. Get me a small nail and a piece of cotton thread." A strange request, but I hastily produced both. A piece of cotton about 15 cm in length was tied to the nail and the pendulum held over each pawpaw plant. Over the female plant the nail rotated clockwise in a circle, over the male plant it oscillated from side to side, and over a neutral plant it remained stationary.

This was my first lesson with the pendulum. I reasoned that if it gave the answer about paw paw then it could be applied to anything else. So I started around the garden with pendulum in hand. What a revelation!

BELOW:
These two plants show evidence of the growth patterns of negative and positive seeds. The small beet on the right (about half the size of the other) was a negative seed.

Why did some lettuce not make hearts? Why was that little cob of corn so thin? Why did the pods of beans vary? Why did a lovely Christmas bush in the garden yield only miserable, pale, undersized flowers. The Christmas bush was a seedling from my previous garden and I could not understand how such a poor flowering tree could come from a beautiful, rich, red, full-flowering parent plant. Now I had the answer: it was the male seed that had grown.

A busy time followed taking out the plants that had never given good results.

Later a science teacher visited the garden. She was thrilled when I showed her what I had learned and advised me to use the scientific names for male and female.

Male — negative
Female — positive
No response — neutral

Ten years of exciting research have followed, hundreds of tests having been made on trees, vegetables, flowers, seeds, soil, etc.

Dowsing, as it is called, is an ancient science and means to seek for something, especially with the aid of a mechanical device such as the pendulum. Water diviners are dowsers and so are those who locate minerals with the aid of a rod. Almost any object suspended on a thread of cotton, fishing line or whatever can be used as a pendulum.

I have used a small shell, key-ring, piece of amethyst, petrified wood, tiger-eye, all with excellent results. At the moment I am using a spring clothes peg in a length of cotton, which works well and has the added advantage that when not in use it can be clipped onto my sleeve or lapel, out of the way but easily accessible.

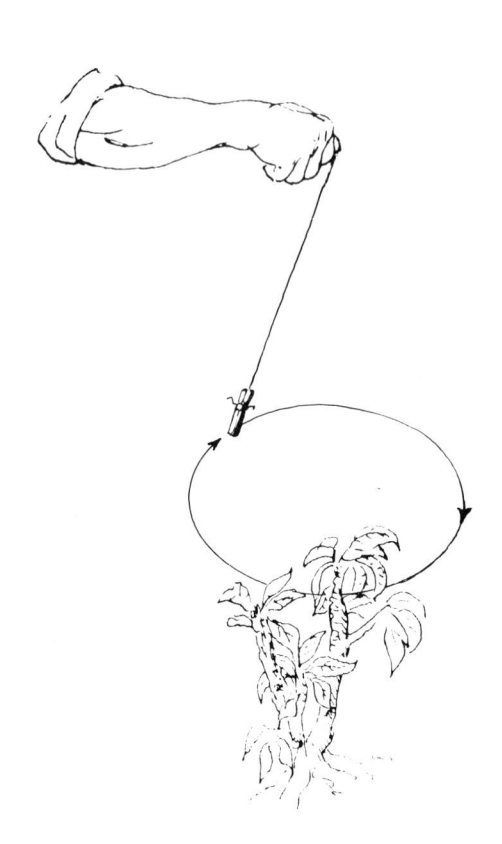

(a) When the pendulum rotates clockwise the plant, seed or soil is POSITIVE

(b) When the pendulum oscillates from side to side, the plant, soil or seed is NEGATIVE

(c) When the pendulum remains stationary, the plant, soil or seed is NEUTRAL

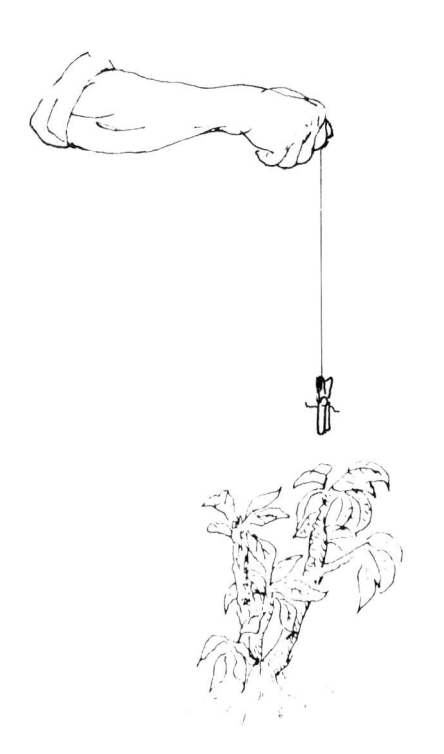

planting

The Soil:

Before planting anything test the soil. Hold a small clod of earth in one hand, suspending the pendulum over it. If it hangs motionless over the clod then the soil has no life force, no humus. Negative soil is indicated when the pendulum oscillates from side to side telling us that the soil needs to be rested.

When the soil has become negative I build another garden on top. The area has not lost future production. In 12 months you should have another bed of fertile, rich soil. If the pendulum gyrates with a circular motion above the clod of earth being tested it is rich in humus and nutriments and ready for immediate use.

The Seeds:

If the soil is ready to receive the seeds, you should determine before planting any of them which are the positive seeds and which the negative. As you would expect, the plants from the positive seeds will be more vigorous and better yielding than those grown from negative seeds. I plant all positive seeds with the occasional negative one put in alongside to test the theory.

To date the pendulum tests have matched the results.

Grow your own seeds:

Allow your best plants to go to seed, but be careful to avoid hybrids. It is so important to use good fertile seeds for successful crops of vegetables. If seed is fertile and falls on fertile soil, it produces a good plant.

REMEMBER: USE THE PENDULUM TO TEST YOUR SEEDS AND PLANT ONLY POSITIVE SEEDS FOR GOOD RESULTS.

BELOW:
Allow some plants to go to seed. You will need to test each seed to find the negative and positive seeds. Not all seeds on the stem are positive or negative.

Ten Different Dahlias from one seed head

Take one seed head of a lovely dahlia, plant the seed and watch for the magic results. The first time I did this it was a thrill to see the variety of colours that came from a lovely pink cactus seed head.

The seeds were planted in my best compost garden. I think every one grew. There seemed too many to put in my garden so I shared some plants with friends asking them to let me see the first flower.

Nine plants were transplanted into good garden; one was left in the original spot and left to grow without help, except, of course, for water.

The plants grew quickly and made wonderful buds. The first flower was a joy to behold. Not one bit like the parent plant. It was the size of a large bread and butter plate of decorative formation. The colour one could scarcely describe. It was in tones from purple to magenta. The tip of the petals were palest mauve and a glow seemed to radiate from it.

One visitor to my garden described this dahlia as having a "halo". Another described it as iridescent. Imagine my joy — 10 different dahlias.

The plants I had shared had created much interest. The most outstanding was a glorious creamy white decorative with pale yellow centre, about 7" across, sitting on a perfectly strong straight stem.

Grow as many of your own vegetable and flower seeds as possible. Choose your very best plant and allow it to mature. Care for it — patience is needed because it takes just on twelve months from seed to seed. That is, from the time you plant your seeds until the time you harvest the seeds.

ABOVE:
This soil is positive. The pendulum is moving in a clockwise direction.

BELOW:
More seed heads from my garden.

4. companion planting & pest control

pest control

As a confirmed adherent of using only natural and organic matter in the garden, the question arises of how we can safely control insects and other pests without resorting to harmful poison sprays and killers. Bounteous Nature has provided us with many safe and effective ways to tackle these problems.

Many varieties of herbs are good repellants of insects and bug pests; by planting them among your vegetables you can control pests as well as having a ready supply of delicious herbs for the table. For example, *garlic* has a pungent aroma which is useful in deterring many flying insects. Rabbits do not like the aroma so keep this in mind if they are a problem for you. Garlic also has the effect of cleaning up the soil and disinfecting it. *Tansy* also deters flying insects so it is useful not only in the vegetable garden, but also placed in a pot on the window sill, or by an open door, it will help to keep flies out of the house. As a bonus, the aroma wafting into the rooms makes them smell much sweeter than any commercially made air fresheners. *Mint* and *sage* when grown close to cabbage will help to protect them from the white cabbage fly. *Thyme* is said to help repel the cabbage root fly. Pennyroyal set on a path will exude a strong tangy aroma when walked upon and if near a door, or preferably on the step, will help to keep insects out of the house.

Marigolds are a first rate insect repellant as well as adding much colour to the vegetable garden and of course will help to bring the bees.

BELOW:
a pot of lemon balm mint adds a wonderful aroma to the garden.

Ed Ramsay

The roots of the French marigold secrete a substance which kills root-eating nematodes. The nematode, or eelworm, is a minutely small creature that can do tremendous damage to the plants in your garden. As well as this valuable function, marigolds among the tomatoes will repel the white fly. *Basil* is also good for keeping disease and pests from tomatoes.

BELOW:
A section of my garden. A mixture of herbs, vegetables and daisies. I grow these in groups rather than rows. This encourages bee activity.

Rosemary repels carrot fly to some extent, however, if this pest is a particular problem onion can be employed as it has a stronger effect.

The slimy slug is attracted to rich soil and compost and what a pest he can be! Of the safe methods of controlling this unwanted and hungry visitor, you can use a strip of sand or sawdust around the vegetables. The slug does not like to walk over the gritty surface, and neither do snails. Another trap for slugs is a hollowed-out half orange peel under which they will gather during the night.

Ed Ramsay

Old cabbage or other vegetable leaves around the edge of the garden provide another favoured hiding place.

In the morning, sprinkle table salt onto the collected slugs to kill them. One of the most effective traps is the old method of putting into the ground an old saucer or a lid of a jar containing a mixture of stale beer and water. Mix the beer and water in equal quantities and be sure that the saucer is pressed into the soil a little so that the slugs can get to it easily. They find this liquid irresistible, and all you have to do is empty the saucer every morning, dispose of the dead slugs, and refill the trap with beer and water. One method I have used extensively in the past to deal with slugs is simply "hunting them down" with a torch at night, picking them off the plants and disposing of them.

Our common hump-back garden snail is actually an import from Asia and not a native species as some people think. Out of its natural environment and away from its natural predators population explosion has taken place as any gardener will tell you. One day some years ago when I was busy in the garden catching snails, I found a new one with a flattish shell which I had not seen before. It was picked up and promptly disposed of along with the hump snails. What a mistake that turned out to be! A few days later I mentioned it to my neighbour who had heard that they were referred to as the Native Snail and that they were cannibals. As you can imagine, my interest was stirred. That evening while searching around the garden with a torch I found a native snail actually eating a hump snail! The two were put into a container and by morning all that remained of the hump snail was a clean shell. Exitedly I made enquiries at The Australia Museum. The snail I had found was Genus Strangesta, Species Capilacea, or the Native Cannibal Snail. Should you be fortunate enough to have such friends in your garden, treasure them. Make sure there's plenty of ground cover and on no account use harmful snail bait. Capilacea like the damp soil under vegetation and

ABOVE:
A native 'cannibal' snail with its spiral shell.

nestle into small hollows often taking their victim with them. They are shiny dark brown in colour, have a thin, flattish shell the underside of which is lighter in colour. The body is dark grey and moves along to the side of the shell. If you do find any in your garden, then feed them on the hump snails and do everything to encourage them.

Another wonderful friend to have is the Leopard Slug. For a long time I killed these creatures. When the cannibal snail episode revealed so much, I felt prompted to question the habits of the leopard slug. Looking back, I realised that I had never once found one on a vegetable plant. They are scavengers, eating only dead food. Five were found eating a rotting orange. They clean up the garden of decaying vegetable matter and do a good job of eating leftover pet's food, bread, etc. Fully grown they can measure up to an incredible 22cm in length. The leopard slug is a valuable helper to have in the garden and you should encourage them by putting out one of their favourite foods, stale wheatmeal biscuits. Always find out the facts about any new creature you find in the garden before destroying it. We can use Nature to fight Nature!

companion planting

Companion Planting is simply placing plants together which like each other's company, in much the same way as we like to have neighbours with whom we are friends, and with whom we get on well. Plants are just the same! Here is a list of plants which do well together, and those which do not.

BELOW:
An upturned ice-cream container reveals the native 'cannibal' snail (top right), and leopard slugs which only cleanse the garden.

Ed Ramsay

ASPARAGUS — likes parsley and tomatoes.

BROAD BEANS — like carrots and cauliflower, red beet, cucumber, cabbage, potatoes, leeks and celery. They don't like members of the onion family.

DWARF AND CLIMBING PEAS — like sweet corn and very much dislike onions, shallots and garlic.

BEET — don't like climbing beans or dwarf beans.

CABBAGE — likes potatoes and herbs, especially sage which also helps to repel pests.

CARROTS — like chives, onions, leeks, sage, peas and lettuce.

CELERY — likes dwarf beans, peas, potato and dill.

CUCUMBER — likes chives, beans, peas, cabbage and potatoes.

GARLIC — hates beans and peas.

KOHLRABI — likes onions and beet, but doesn't like climbing beans.

LEEKS — like celery.

LETTUCE — likes carrots and radishes.

ONIONS — like the influence of carrots.

PARSLEY — likes asparagus and tomatoes.

PEAS — like turnips, beans, sweet corn, radishes, carrots, cucumbers, but hate the onion family.

POTATO — likes beans, peas, sweet corn, cabbage, but dislikes tomatoes and sunflowers.

PUMPKIN — dislikes potatoes but does enjoy the company of sweet corn.

RADISH — likes most plants in the garden.

TOMATOES — like parsley, asparagus and basil but dislike kohlrabi and potatoes.

SWEDES AND TURNIPS — like peas.

The chances of your success will be greatly improved if you keep this list in mind when planting. It can be seen from the accompanying photograph that the peas climbing on the bottom right hand side of the trellis are discoloured. I was puzzled as to why those on that side were sick, until I realised that they were suffering from the influence of the onions planted near them. Those on the far side away from the onions were doing well. Since the photo was taken, I have moved the oinions and the peas are now doing well again. So plant your vegetables among their friends.

BELOW:
Parsley growing happily with the cabbages.

Ed Ramsay

the earthworm

I must mention another friend to all gardens and gardeners, whom we are apt sometimes to forget. He is the earthworm who can help you to achieve amazing results. Earthworms will burrow tirelessly in the soil creating tiny tunnels which carry water down to the plants' roots and so decrease runoff in heavy rain. He eats fungi and harmful insect eggs as well as leaving a "cast" from the soil passing through the digestive system. This is a valuable additional fertiliser. Even when life is over, the decaying worms yield a source of fertiliser which is very rich in nitrogen. Worms are essential in the compost heap and if conditions are right they will breed there waiting to be "transplanted" into your garden, where they contribute greatly to the health of soil and plants.

Naturally, healthy plants are more immune to disease and pest attack than sick ones and this is Nature's way of ensuring that only the best survive. Make sure that all your plants are healthy survivors by simply creating the right conditions for them naturally, and you can eat your way to health and happiness with home grown foods.

BELOW:
Onions planted near these peas are gradually killing them.

5. comfrey & other herbs

"He causeth the grass to grow for the cattle and the herb for the service of man." (Psalm 104:14)

comfrey

Comfrey — the miracle herb — has been known, used in many ways and sold for hundreds of years. Ancient physicians called it Knit Bone because of its remarkable healing properties. In more recent times, much research has been directed to finding out more about this miracle herb. The Henry Doubleday Research Foundation in the United Kingdom has been a leader in the discovery of the myriad of qualities of the plant. No garden is complete without Comfrey.

Comfrey belongs to the Borage family and is a native of Europe. Because it is a vigorous grower that does well in most soil and climatic conditions, it is now widely propagated in many parts of the world. Its deep roots grow down into the subsoil bringing to the surface minerals and nutrients unavailable to plants with a shallower root system. The plant grows 1½-2 metres in height and has thick, prolific, furry leaves. Both the roots of the plant and the leaves are beneficial to us as well as to other plants, as I have mentioned in the section on fertilizers. The plant, when well developed, will divide readily and produce seed heads, the flowers are delicately pinky mauve or white. Odd seeds will sometimes self-sow, but I feel that better results can be obtained by propagating the plant from pieces of the comfrey root.

The abundant leaf growth can be used in many ways. As a green manure, chop the leaves up and lightly turn them into the topsoil around plants. Quick decomposition will free nitrogen from the leaves and the topsoil will be enriched with calcium and other minerals.

BELOW:
A rich crop of corn.

The comfrey leaves make an excellent herbal tea. It is used as a blood cleanser, is good for teeth and bones and is a cell proliferant. Comfrey speeds up the rate at which the body replace sold cells with new ones, hence the old name of Knit Bone. The miracle healing properties of the herb are due to the active ingredient which is scientifically known as Allantoin. It is used as an ingredient in skin ointments for the treatment of burns, wounds, etc.

BELOW:
Comfrey. The plant grows to about 2 metres high and has thick furry leaves.

The comfrey root is also used in ointments and in tablet form. Comfrey is the only plant that contains Vitamin B-12, and as well is a rich source of natural calcium and other minerals, plus chlorophyll. The early matured spring growth of the root can be dried and is available commercially from health food stores.

Several leaves steamed, chopped finely and sprinkled with a little lemon jiuce and oil, make an excellent hot vegetable which is helpful in restoring tissue damage. The very young leaves can be used in salads.

Comfrey tea is a wonderful pick-up drink and easy to make. Take 6 medium sized leaves, wash well, cut up well and cover with 1½ pints of boiling water. Allow to brew, just like regular tea, and serve hot with a little lemon juice and honey to taste. Alternatively, it can be served cold with fruit juice added. A glass full of cold comfrey tea flavoured with black currant juice makes a drink fit for a king.

Comfrey leaves put through a juice extractor give a thick green juice which is very beneficial when used as a poultice to renew and repair bruises, sprains and damaged surface tissue. The leaves after being crushed or heated with a little boiling water, can be applied straight to the skin on a bandage or cotton wool. Cover this poultice with a piece of plastic and then bind over the pad with another bandage. Care should be taken to avoid contact with clothing or bed linen as it will leave a brown stain which is difficult to remove. Such a poultice is reputed to be of benefit when treating tennis elbow, or other strains resulting from vigorous sport.

Compost making benefits by the use of old comfrey leaves, and a nourishing liquid fertilizer can also be made with the leaves. For complete information, see the section on Fertilizers.

Pieces of root 3 cm to 6 cm in length, planted about 6 cm into the soil, will soon give new comfrey plants. Give the young plants plenty of sunshine and moisture, and a place to grow where they can multiply without encroaching on other plants. They will give you a harvest of goodness for the whole family. Comfrey dies down during the winter, but will quickly make spring growth if kept mulched and given a dose of seaweed liquid or good compost. Unfortunately, the seeds seem to be unavailable, or at least I have never been able to locate a place that can supply them. Some nurseries stock the roots, or one of your friends might have enough to share.

other herbs

All herbs are a real delight to have in the garden. It is a good idea to grow them among your vegetables. They can increase the interest in your food and cooking with their delicious flavours, and the health of the garden with their beneficial effect on other plants and ability to repel insect pests.

Borage, the "herb of gladness", is a particular favourite of mine. Tea made with borage leaves is very good for you, and the smallish leaves dipped in light batter and fried in vegetable oil are a delicious entree to serve at your next dinner party. The bees in the garden are attracted to this delightful plant — how they love the little blue flowers — and its presence will therefore promote pollination in the garden.

Here is a list of some of the common herbs, their properties and uses.

BASIL is a beautifully strong-smelling herb which loves to grow in strong sunshine. Grow it and eat it with tomatoes. When cooking with it, add the herb only at the last minute.

BORAGE flowers and leaves can be used in salads, but take care to chop the leaves very finely, as they are hairy. It is said to have a cheering effect on the mind and heart.

CHAMOMILE is soothing for upset stomachs and for babies who are having teething problems. The tea is made from the flower heads.

CHIVES have an antiseptic action like all the onion family and hence are said to help prevent disease. Marvellous in omelettes, potato salads, anywhere a mild onion taste is required. ONION and GARLIC are part of the same family of herbs.

COMFREY has been discussed in the text.

CORIANDER leaves and tiny fruit are used for flavouring. It is said to be a stimulant and a carminative.

DANDELION stimulates the liver and promotes gall-cleansing. It is wonderful added to salads.

DILL. Make soothing dill-water for treatment of indigestion. Soak a teaspoonful of bruised seeds in 3 cups of cold water for about 6 to 8 hours. Strain and sweeten with honey, giving a dose of 1 tablespoonful to adults and 1 teaspoonful to children. Use the leaves when cooking fish.

EAU-DE-COLOGNE MINT should be kept in the bathroom or airless, stuffy rooms to sweeten the air. Chew to sweeten the breath.

Basil

Fenel Seed

Caraway

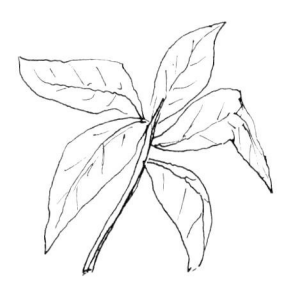

Bay Leaf

LEMON BALM makes a beautiful tea, which is said to lift the spirits when one is feeling tired, depressed. Bees are attracted to it in the garden.

MARJORAM is a culinary herb as well as a tonic. It goes well with tomato dishes.

MINT is one of the most famous herbs of all time. Everyone knows how good mint sauce is with spring lamb! It is said also to be good for the mind and memory.

PARSLEY contains Vitamin A and C, iron, calcium and phosphorus. It is good for the kidneys and nerves.

PENNYROYAL is a dwarf mint with a strong flavour. Use a little in teas or drinks. It likes being walked on, and exudes a strong aroma when bruised. Grow near the door, in pots preferably on the step. Will help to repel ants and fleas.

PEPPERMINT is a popular herbal tea, high in Vitamin C and is good for colds, flu and upset stomachs.

SAGE leaves added to normal tea will strengthen resistance to disease. Gargle with the cold tea for relief from sore throats.

TANSY should be planted in a pot and kept near doorways and windows to help repel flies.

THYME is good when added to stuffings, meatloaves and other meat dishes, imparting a strong and pleasant taste.

YARROW is a general strengthener and has been used by the Chinese for thousands of years. Helps to prevent colds.

Grow herbs in your garden because a garden without fragrance is a garden without soul.

Majoram

Oregano

Parsley

Sage

A KISS OF THE SUN FOR
PARDON THE
SONG OF THE BIRD FOR
MIRTH
ONE IS NEARER GODS HEART
IN A GARDEN
THAN ANYWHERE ELSE
ON EARTH.

CHINESE CAB.
FOR SEED

6. fertilizing, compost & home made liquids

compost

Compost is essential to making and retaining a good vegetable garden. IT IS NATURE'S SUPREME FERTILIZER! Good compost is filled with every good organic material, minerals, millions of helpful micro-organisms as well as trace elements. Soils rich in organic matter are a breeding ground for some of the helpful bacteria and moulds which attack many of the fungi that produce plant disease. If you haven't been using lots of compost in your garden then both you and your plants have been missing out badly. This is particularly important when growing vegetables, since the more healthy the plant is, the more healthy you will be for having eaten it.

In a correctly made compost heap, Nature does all of the work for you, your only task being to provide the right conditions. Many things can go into the compost heap: any green plant matter (provided it is free from disease), lawn clippings, kitchen waste, fruit and vegetable peelings, weeds, seaweed, vines of peas and beans and so on. In a properly made heap the temperature will rise to about 180°F, and it is then that bacteria will break down and decay the vegetable matter. After some time the heap will cool and our friends the earthworms will move in, redistributing the material and "cultivating" the heap. After about 8 months you will have a treaure trove of organic goodness.

The heap will rot down better and faster if you use some type of activator, such as animal or bird manure.

BELOW:
Rich, sweet-smelling compost. Seeds planted in compost grow quicker and the plants are healthier.

Ed Ramsay

"The top of the bin is covered by a hinged wooden lid."

"Air holes are a necessity in the walls"

"two openings in the front wall each 15 inches wide."

"There must be earth contact with the compost."

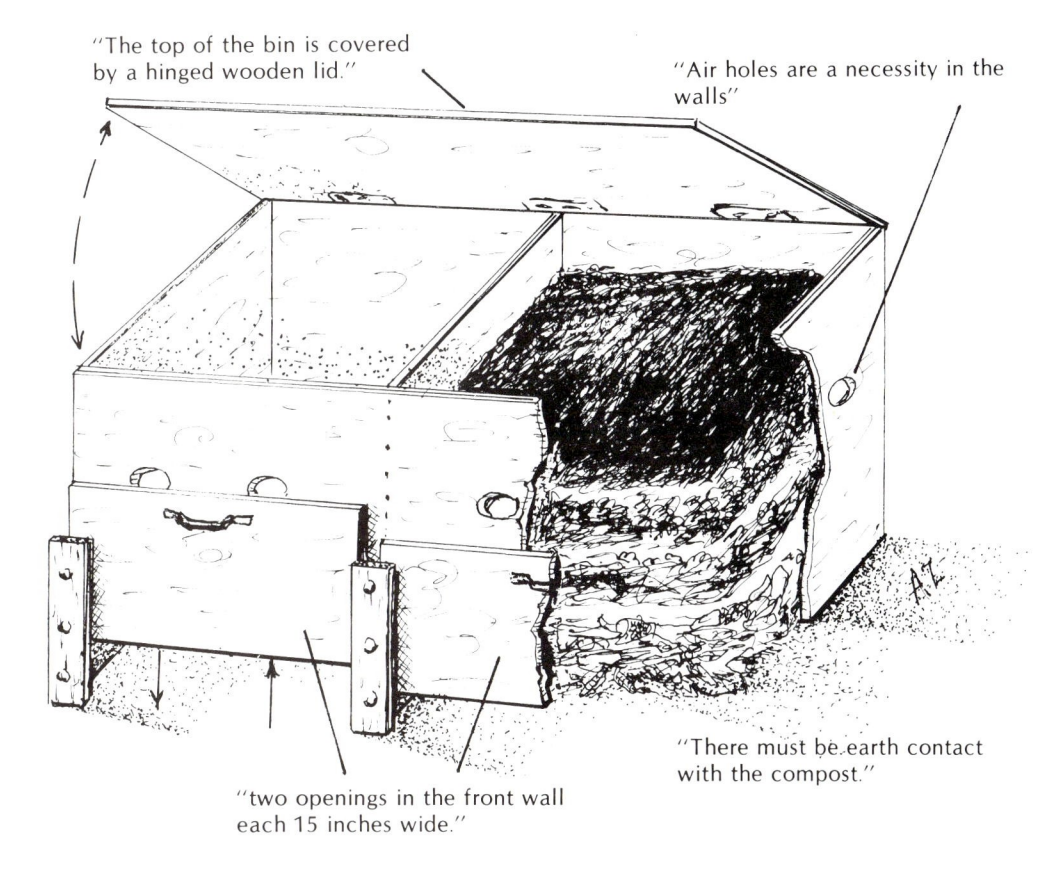

"The advantage of a large bin is that it does give plenty of good compost after 8 or 9 months, and allows you to be refilling one side while still using the already composted material which you have pushed over to the other."

Blood and bone is excellent for this purpose, while some people use fish meal, if they have a ready source of supply. Comfrey leaves are a wonderful addition to the compost heap and should be used whenever possible.

The most important factor in the construction of the compost bin is that the bottom of the bin must be open. There must be earth contact with the compost. I believe that magnetic rays, radiation and other forces come through the bottom of the bin to aid in the rotting process and help produce a really first class result. Whether you purchase one of the commercially made bins, or build your own, it must be bottomless.

My own compost bin measures 6 feet long by 5 feet wide, and is 3 feet high. It has concrete walls approximately 3 inches thick and two openings in the front wall each 15 inches wide. A piece of hardboard which slides down from the top of the bin on the inside prevents the compost from spilling out. The top of the bin is covered by a hinged wooden lid. Air holes are a necessity in the walls and in my bin there are about 8 holes, each the size of a half-brick. Without air, the compost will smell sour.

Use whatever materials are available to you when building a bin, but remember that air holes and earth contact are necessary. The advantage of a large bin is that it does give plenty of good compost after 8 or 9 months, and allows you to be refilling one side while still using the already composted material which you have pushed over to the other.

When filling the bin, the first layer should be of coarse cuttings such as hydrangea, sweet corn stalks, choko vine or stalks, old bean plant (use only clean material) to a depth of about 25 cm. Tread this down moderately firmly and if the material is a little dry add a little water. On top of this pile about 20 cm of weeds, autumn leaves, lawn clippings, vegetable peelings, seaweed etc. Next sprinkle a few handfulls of blood and bone, poultry manure, or whatever activator you choose. On top of this another 25 cm layer of garden and kitchen refuse and so on until the heap has reached the required height. Don't forget to separate the layers of refuse with manure and a little lime powder or dolomite. Keep the layers level because the bacteria work horizontally and the earthworms vertically. Finally on the very top of the heap sprinkle a layer about 5 or 6 cm deep of good soil or sand to help retain the heat. Water the heap initially and thereafter keep it just moist. Lift the lid now and again, if your bin has one, to allow rain and sunshine onto the compost. The rain adds minerals and the sunshine will sweeten the mixture.

I have never found it necessary to turn the heap; I think that it rots better if you leave it alone. Once the heap has become very hot due to the action of the bacteria, and then cooled right back, the earthworms will invade it and do the turning for you. When the compost is ready to be used it is sweet smelling crumbly black or dark brown soil, showing no traces of the original materials. If your compost looks and feels allright, but has a sour smell, the problem has been a lack of air. In the next binful you make, it will be a good idea to make air holes by pushing a crowbar or pipe into the mix in three or four places.

Compost is critical to the success of the NO-DIG GARDEN. It can also be spread around shrubs and other plants to give them nourishment. The earthworms which have bred happily in the heap while it was forming will now be transferred to the garden where they will pull the compost down greatly enriching the soil.

BELOW:
flowers in bloom, plants going to seed, vegetables and herbs all prospering together.

Ed Ramsay

liquid fertilizer

The other three fertilizers I have always used are homemade liquid fertilizers. They are comfrey liquid, poultry liquid, and seaweed liquid.

Comfrey liquid fertilizer is made by taking an old metal drum, or plastic garbage container of about 10 gallons capacity and packing it half full with *large* comfrey leaves. Then fill the container to the brim with water and leave it to soak for 3 weeks, until the leaves have rotted down. This stock liquid is mixed 50/50 with water and poured around the roots of the plants.

The *poultry manure* liquid fertilizer is made in the same way. Using a drum of the same capacity, half fill it with the manure and top up with water. Allow this one to stand for 4 weeks and use well diluted; the ideal strength in my experience is 1 pint of the stock solution to 1 bucketfull (2 gallons) of water. Again, pour it around the roots of the plants.

The *seaweed* liquid is made by half filling the drum with seaweed, topping it up with water and allowing it to stand for about 3 months. The beautiful rich liquid is very strong and must be very much diluted before use. Too strong a solution will cause "burning" of the roots of the plant. The ideal dilution is ½ a cup of stock solution to a bucket of water, or 4 fl.oz. per 2 gallons.

The comfrey liquid can be used for pot plants if it is super-diluted. I have found that about 1 fl.oz. of the stock solution added to a gallon of water makes a nourishing mixture. Regular application of this liquid, plus plenty of sunlight and love will make your indoor plants thrive.

BELOW:
crinkly lettuce is an important vegetable in my salad garden.

Acknowledgements

Thanks to the numerous people who have contributed by sharing the garden and for the success that many have enjoyed with the 'No-Dig' Garden.

My special thanks to Vivian Malfroy, Ruth Swan, Jeanette Percy, John Miller and Christopher Atkins.

Also to Ed Ramsay and Dan Thatcher, for the use of their photographs.